3

Black Sea

Caucas
Mount.
rang

Turkey

Aegean
Sea

Mediterranean
Sea

Egypt

Arabi

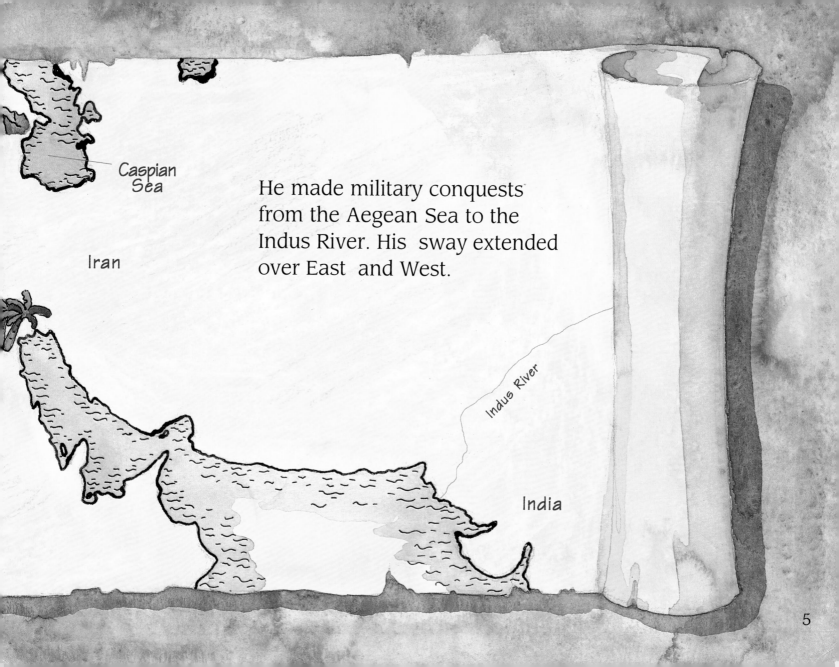

Caspian
Sea

Iran

He made military conquests
from the Aegean Sea to the
Indus River. His sway extended
over East and West.

Indus River

India

5

He was just and righteous, protecting the
weak and punishing the law-breakers.

When Dhul Qarnayan took his armies to the North-East of Iran, he reached the Caucasus mountain range which runs between the Caspian and the Black Seas.

8

On these journeys he met different tribes in different places. Once he met a tribe whose members were hardly able to communicate with him.

11

Once, in that region, he met a tribe who begged him to protect them from the wild tribes, the Yajuj and the Majuj (Gog and Magog) who kept coming through the mountain passes, and attacking them.

13

Dhul Qarnayan said, "Lend me a body of men, and I will raise a wall between you and them. Come, bring me blocks of iron."

He told them to ply their bellows
and when the iron blocks which
they brought became red hot, Dhul
Qarnayan asked them to pour
molten brass on them.

17

18

In this way he helped in damming up the valley between the two mountains.

20

In this way, Dhul Qarnayan erected an Iron Wall to save them from Yajuj and Majuj.

After conquering a major part of the then inhabited world and building an iron wall, Dhul Qarnayan lost none of his humility.

He gave the entire credit for these feats to the blessing of Allah. Of the iron wall he had built, he said:

"This is a blessing from my Lord. But when the promise of my Lord will come to pass, He will make it to dust. And the promise of my Lord is true."

Find Out More
To know more about the message and meaning of Allah's words, look up the following parts of the Quran which tell the story of the King Dhul Qarnayan.
Surah al-Kahf 18:83-98

24